Not My Son,
Not on
Mother's Day

Not My Son, Not on Mother's Day

Theresa Dove-Waters

ISBN: 978-1-64871-688-1   (Paperback Edition)
ISBN: 978-1-64871-689-8   (Hardcover Edition)
ISBN: 978-1-64871-687-4   (E-book Edition)

Book Ordering Information

Phone Number: 347-901-4929 or 347-901-4920
Email: info@globalsummithouse.com
Global Summit House
www.globalsummithouse.com

Printed in the United States of America

CONTENTS

ACKNOWLEDGMENTS

To God for Divine Grace, my deceased mother, Catherine Smith, my beloved deceased husband Leander Waters, my sons Anthony and Jeffery.

CHAPTER ONE

Not on Mother's Day

"Mama, mama, wake up... I need to talk to you." My eyes began to open slowly. I wasn't sure if I was dreaming or someone was calling my name. *Why was the room so dark? Who is that standing over my bed?* The shadow appeared to be that of an older adult, and his shoulders were humped over. "Mama, are you awake? I need to talk to you!" *What time is it? It must still be nighttime because I can't see . . . is that Jeff? Yes, it's Jeff!* My heart began to race. I could hear the thumping of my heart. The empty feeling in the pit of my stomach was taking control of my body. Fear gripped my entire body and soul. I wanted to go back to sleep and never wake up. "Mama, do you hear me?" I began to pray, "Lord, what can it be this time?" *Had he been in a car accident?*

Maybe someone was on the phone. Please, Lord, don't let it be bad news. "Mama, I need to talk to you!" *Maybe if I keep my eyes closed, he will go away.*

"Yes, Jeff, what is it? Give me a minute to turn on the light," I finally said. I slowly began to make an effort to gather my thoughts. For just a moment, I didn't recognize this 6' 4" young man standing over me. His eyes were glazed over, and his face said that he was much older than his 17 years. Yet, at the same time, he appeared to be a little boy who needed help getting on his bicycle. I could not remember the last time that he had asked for help from me.

I took a deep breath, trying to control my body before having to react to yet another of Jeff's situations. In a voice that was trembling from fear, finally, I said, "Yes, what is it?"

"I'm in trouble."

"What kind of trouble are you in?"

"It's serious this time."

"Yes, go on."

"I need help."

"What kind of help do you need?"

"I need to go into a drug treatment center."

"Why?"

"Mama, I'm afraid. I need help!"

"Do you mean that you have been drinking again? You've only been going to the counselor for two weeks about your drinking. We need to give it more time."

"Mama, you don't understand it's much more than drinking, it's serious."

In a faint voice, I was able to muster up a comment that would allow me to stall.

"I don't believe that we can get you into a treatment center… remember, I called and was told that the insurance company would not pay for in-patient treatment. Besides, I do believe that if you try, you can stop drinking. It's not that difficult, especially if you stop hanging around with the wrong crowd."

"Mama, stop and listen to me, please. Help me. It's much more than drinking."

"OK, OK, go back to bed, and I promise that I will work something out tomorrow."

As our eyes locked, it was as if we were looking into the depths of each other's souls. I could almost read his mind. *I've hurt her again.* Could he read my thoughts? I hoped not, because I would never want him to know my inner thoughts. I would not want him to see the rage that I'm feeling from having to deal with this substance problem. After all, a mother is supposed to stand by her children. I shall never forget the relief in his eyes as he turned and walked away. He's no doubt thinking - she'll *work it out. She always does. I can depend on her.* I could hear him slowly closing his bedroom door. *Now, what do I do? I don't have time to focus on the past; what do I do about the promise that I had just made?*

The clock revealed that it was 2:00 am. The tears began to flow, and the prayers started. My prayer was short and to the point. "Lord, it's me again, and it's about Jeff once again. Please direct me to a treatment center that will take my son. Help me to help my son." For the first time in several days, my body became somewhat calm. The last seven days had been a living hell. For the first time in 17 years, I was fearful. His behavior had taken a turn for the worst slamming doors, shouting and walking back and forth. I also remembered the handgun that I found under his mattress as I searched for clues. The night before, there had been a shouting match between the two of us, because I turned a young man away from the door who asked if he could talk with Jeff.

Who was the young man? I had never seen him before, and I was not about to call Jeff to the door. Besides, he was sleeping, and I hoped that he would sleep throughout the night. As luck would have it, just as I closed the door, he came out of his room and asked who was at the door? He became agitated when I informed him that I told the young man that he was asleep. There was a sense of urgency in his voice. "How could you do that? I needed to talk to him!" Even to this day, I shudder every time I think about that night. He began to cry and pace back and forth. "Mama, how could you do that?" *What was the big deal?*

Here it is three hours later, and reality began to set in. The tears continued to flow. How would I be able to keep my promise? I had tried to get help for him earlier in the month for his drinking problem. I still didn't want to believe that he was drinking too much, although he suggested that sometimes he had a little too much. What other reason would there be for him to get into trouble in and out of school? A school counselor recommended that I bring him in for counseling, and after an initial assessment, the recommended was that he and I come in for counseling sessions.

During the sessions, he laid it on thick; he told her about his running with the wrong crowd and swore that he wanted to change his ways and get away from that group. After several sessions, the counselor recommended that he take a drug called-Antabuse. The counselor would administer the drug after each session. Antabuse is a drug that will make a person violently sick if alcohol is drunk when taking the medication. After he started taking the medication, I felt relieved. *Maybe this is the answer. Besides, his drinking problem was* mostly due to peer pressure.

After he started taking the Antabuse, I became suspicious one day when we arrived for a counseling session. We were getting out of the car, and as we passed each other, our faces almost touched. The smell of alcohol was in the air. *Has he been drinking? I saw him take the medication.* I remembered thinking, *don't be so suspicious give him a chance. Besides, this time he seems to be sincere.*

That was several months ago. Now I must return to reality. I tried to gather my thoughts quickly and get back to the task at hand. Just a few hours ago, it was Mother's Day, and I cherished the card that Jeff gave me. I was surprised, especially since we had been at each other's throat all week. The hand-written note at the end of the message was encouraging. In his own words:

Mama, stop worrying, you'll be happy one day.

It was now 6:00 am. I needed a few more minutes of sleep before sorting all of this out. No, I had to get up and deal with this now. *Where is the telephone book? Hopefully, I can discover a treatment center in the area.* I could not hold back the tears; *why did I have to move? Maybe if I had stayed in Jacksonville around family and friends, none of this would have happened. My mother told me not to move to Georgia. Perhaps it's Anthony's fault. Did he have to leave home and join the Air Force? Didn't he realize that I had always depended on him to take care of his little brother? Damn it! Wasn't I a good mother?*

I'll try this one; it's only thirty minutes away. It's worth a try. I'll call around nine. I wonder if he's sleeping? Yes, he was asleep. It had been years since I peeked in to check on him. *A cup of coffee will help me wake up.*

9 am, I dialed the toll-free number to the treatment center, and a woman answered the phone. "Yes, may I help you?" I almost hung up. *Why even try? Well, what do I have to lose?* "Yes, I need to talk to someone about my son. I think he has a drinking problem." "Yes, ma'am, let me connect you to a counselor." The young man, on the other end, was very empathetic as I told him our story. When I finished, he inquired about my insurance information. I began to pray. "Lord, this is an emergency; I've come to a dead end." The young man's voice brought me back to reality. "Ma'am, your insurance will not pay for in-patient treatment." My heart began to sink.

Upon seeing my despair, he replied, "however, if you think that your son is in danger of harming himself or someone else, the insurance company will pay for a 30-day emergency stay."

"Yes! Yes! I believe that he will harm himself. His behavior has changed, and there was a gun under his bed. I don't want to lose my son. Yes, I am afraid that he may harm himself."

"Well, based on that, you can bring him in. Can you get here by 2 pm?"

"Yes, yes, we will be there."

As I pulled into the driveway, I began to sob, **"Thank you, Lord, Thank you, Lord, Thank You, Lord!"** "Jeff, get up I need to talk with you. I need you to come into the living room so we can talk. It can't wait. Get up! I'll get some coffee while you get dressed." As I walked past the table that displayed family photos, I glanced at the photographs of both my sons and wondered when did things change? It had been just the three of us. What happened to our close family? We had so much fun, the little league football games, the excitement of baking cookies, and opening one gift on Christmas Eve. It all seemed so very long ago, or was it?

As he entered the room, he sat down and looked as if he was still in a daze. "I was able to talk with someone at a treatment center in Macon, and they want us to come in at two."

"Jeff, now tell me what's going on. Earlier, you said that it's dangerous. Tell me more. Are you doing hard drugs?

"Yes."

"Who are you getting them from?"

"Mama, you don't know him."

"But tell me!"

"It's the guy who drives the Corvette."

"You have got to be kidding; he appears to be much older than you and such a nice guy. I'm going to call the policeman who lives two houses down the street and ask him to come over. Where is the phone book?"

Found it! "Hello, this is Mrs. Dove. I work at the college. Yes, I know we've met before. Can you come over? My son and I need to talk to you. It's important."

As we sat waiting, it seemed like hours, and I had this damn lump in my throat that would not go away. I did not want to start crying again. *Why would an adult sell drugs to a high school kid? Well, I can't wait to report his ass.* Just as I was getting more agitated, there was a knock on the door. The officer looked as if he had just gotten out of bed. "Yes, ma'am, what can I do for you?" "We want to report a drug dealer to you. He has been selling my son drugs. Jeff, you tell him."

The officer didn't seem surprised with the very detailed account of the drug activity that was going on, nor was he taken aback by the name of the person selling drugs. His response shocked the socks off me. Standing up and turning as red as a firecracker, he shouted, "I told that SOB if he ever sold drugs to school kids that I would get his ass, especially boys on the football team. Ms. Dove, I'll check into the matter." "Yes, you do just that." As he approached the door, he said to Jeff, "You are doing a fine job on the football team. We are sure glad that you and your mom moved to this town."

When the policeman left, I told Jeff that he had to get dressed. Since I wasn't sure where I was going, we needed to leave as soon as possible. Although it was only thirty miles away, the drive seemed endless. Neither of us said very much. What was there to say? I did not want to share my true feelings. I was afraid that my anger would be a catalyst for another fight. When would the fighting stop?

Here we are in a new town, a new state and my hopes that things will get better have almost vanished. Lord knows I don't want my colleagues over at the college to know that my son is out of control. Drinking, and maybe drugs, and now we are on our way to a treatment center. *Perhaps if he can get the drinking under control, things will get back to normal. Surely, he is not that involved in drugs; where would he get the money to buy drugs? Several people told me that most young men smoke marijuana once in a while. Maybe he shouldn't be going to a drug treatment center. After all, he isn't a drug addict. Well, it will not harm to have an assessment done by a substance abuse counselor.*

CHAPTER TWO

Who Stole My Joy?

"Yes, may I help you?"

"Yes, I'm Ms. Dove, and this is my son Jeffrey; we have an appointment."

"Yes, the counselor will be with you in just a short while. Please fill out these forms for me, May I make a copy of your insurance card?"

Well, this seems like a beautiful place. It's nice and clean. I am so tired; my entire body is aching and tense.

"Ms. Dove, will you and your son like to have something to drink?"

"No, thanks."

"Hi, Ms. Dove, my name is Mr. Jack. Please come in."

Why is this room so small? The three of us can barely sit in here.

"What seems to be the problem?"

"Well, I talked with you this morning about my son. I think he has a slight drinking problem. He is seeing a counselor and is taking Antabuse, but earlier this morning, he said that he needed to come to a treatment center, something about drugs."

Why is he smiling? Maybe he is too young to be a drug counselor; I don't see anything funny about this!

"Ms. Dove, let's hear from Jeffrey. Jeffrey, what's going on?"

"Well, it's like this . . . I told my mom that I've been drinking and doing drugs."

"What type of drugs?"

"Well, I've been smoking marijuana."

"Anything else?"

What does he mean anything else?

"Yes, I've done other drugs, now what?"

Here we go again. Another surprise go-ahead and steals my joy. You get pleasure out of ruining my day; why should today be any different? Who is this child?

"Well, it's cocaine!" *What the hell is he talking about, cocaine! How would he know what cocaine is? I don't even know what cocaine is. How do you use it? Didn't I read somewhere that cocaine can damage the brain?*

I tried to open my mouth, but nothing came out. The lump in my throat had gotten larger. *Lord, help me to speak.* At that moment, a strange voice came out of the mouth, and I said, "Cocaine?" "Yes, Mama, cocaine." The counselor looked him square in the eyes.

"How long have you been using cocaine?"

"For about two months."

"What about drinking? When did you start drinking?"

"I was fourteen."

My God, Jeff, did you say fourteen? Where did you get the alcohol? The lump finally vanished, and I began to sob as never before. As Mr. Jack stood and walked over to put his arm around my shoulders, I could sense the maturity in his hands.

"Ms. Dove, will you come with me next door? I know that this is a shock for you."

"Did you hear him say that he started drinking at fourteen?"

"Yes, ma'am, I heard him. Some kids start much younger. Parents may be caught off guard when they learn that their child started drinking at a young age. We have treated kids as young as ten years old. On the phone, you said that you thought that Jeff might be in danger of harming himself."

"Yes."

"Tell me about that."

"Well, the other night, I found a gun under his mattress, and I'm afraid that he will harm himself."

"We are going to admit him on an emergency basis, but before we do, I need to talk with him, and then we will begin the intake process. Will you be OK in here?"

My head felt like a ton of brick as I nodded yes. *OK . . . will I be OK? How could he ask such a dumb question? My whole world has just caved in on me, and you ask if I will be OK.*

After the door closed, the floodgate opened. There was no need to pretend that everything was OK. I just wanted to cry without being ashamed, no apology needed, no explanation, no cover-up, no pretending, no fear, hurt, guilt, just tears.

Lord, how did we get here? Where did I go wrong? A fourteen-year-old kid drinking alcohol? And now, yes, maybe even cocaine. Surely there would have been some sign. Well, maybe there were early warnings, and I didn't want to admit to them. I remember very clearly, several years ago, just before Anthony left for the Air Force, Jeffrey called; he was at the skating rink and called home for his brother to come and get him. When they drove into the carport, I could hear a noise outside. As I walked out, I was shocked to see Jeffrey leaning over and vomiting from the back seat of the car.

"Mama, don't get excited, he had a few drinks with another boy," Anthony said.

"Jeff, have you been drinking?"

"Yes, Dewayne gave me something to drink, and my head is just about to split. I will never take another drink in my life!"

"Have you ever had a drink before?"

"No, Mama."

I thought maybe that would teach him a lesson. I'm sure that he won't drink again. Boys will be boys. Besides, it's the kid down the street. I'm not so sure about him. Maybe I'll talk with Jeff about hanging around with the wrong crowd. He's coming of age now, so it's time for a talk about peer pressure. Sure wish that there was a man that I could turn to, someone who could mentor Jeff. It's rough being a single parent. Oh well, you do what you have to do.

This room feels so secure. It would be nice to stay here for two or three days away from the outside world. I wonder what they are talking about doing? How long will it take to do an intake?

I can't remember if we ever had that talk about peer pressure? I couldn't remember, but I knew that his behavior flared and flayed out of control after that night he came home from the skating rink. There was also the time when I had to go out of town for an all-day conference. I don't believe he went to school that day. When I returned home, I noticed that an empty wine bottle was on the pool table (part of my Christmas stash). "Jeff, what happened to this bottle of wine?" "Oh, that bottle?" "Well, I was reaching into the cabinet, and it fell, but the bottle didn't break; the top wasn't on tight, and it spilled all over the floor." To this day, I can't believe that I was dumb enough to buy that story! At the same time, I began to get more calls from the school. . . Jeffrey was not attending classes. Jeffrey was fighting in school one conference after another.

During Middle school, all hell broke loose. I remember his sixth-grade teacher, a young white woman who had just graduated from college. It was her first year on the job and the earlier stages of school integration. To this day, I wonder if she continued to teach after that half-year of having Jeffrey in her class. Almost daily, I would get a telephone call. "Ms. Dove, this is Ms. Perry, I need you to come to the school for a parent /teacher conference." "Yea, Yea, I will get there in the morning. Ms. Perry, can you give me a clue as to what to expect? What happened today?"

Jeffrey, I got a call today from Ms. Perry. She said that you would not pay attention or stay in your seat. "Mama, I told you she doesn't like me." "Jeff, listen, I have to work, and I cannot continue to leave work or go in late because of conferences with your teachers. You either get with it or else."

I thought to myself. *I know what the problem is; he's trying to intimidate Ms. Perry.* I still chuckle at the time when I had him sit on the floor and look up at me when I was talking to him. He was trying to intimidate me. Subsequently, I had to take this action: When he became taller than I, he would stand up when I chastised him. He was 5'10" tall, and I was 5'4". Having him sit on the floor looking up at me sure got his attention (sometimes I'm a little slow in getting the message).

The straw that broke the camel's back that year was when I received a call to go to the school to meet with the principal and the school counselor. The principal initiated the discussion, "Ms. Dove, we need to talk with you about Jeff's behavior. We have been charting his behavior, and it appears that he may have some behavior disorder. We want to do further assessments. It may be necessary for us to get special assistance to him." "What do you mean, special assistance?" "Well, if our suspicions pan out, he could be placed in a "behavior disorder classroom." "Are you talking about special education?" "Well, yes." "No way! I am very familiar with how Black males are placed into behavior disorder classrooms when young white teachers can't manage their classes. You do not have my permission to test him for special education? *If anything, he is misbehaving because he misses his brother.*

Well, that was then; the counselor sure has been in there with him for a long time. Maybe things aren't as gruesome as they seemed an hour ago; at least I've stopped crying. But if today is anything like most other days, the tears will return, if not today, tomorrow.

The counselor interrupted my thoughts, "Ms. Dove, we are ready to get Jeffrey checked in. I will be back in a few minutes, and we will talk." *Why is he looking at me with such compassion? I wonder if he realizes the agony that I've been through, or should I say we have all been through my mother, Anthony, and yes, even Jeff.. the hurts, fears, and guilt.*

When the counselor came back, he smiled as he came towards me. "Ms. Dove, we have checked Jeffrey into his room. You will not be able to have contact with him for ten days. In the meantime, we also have a program here for family members. There are group sessions once a week, and you will be required to attend the sessions; its part of Jeffrey's recovery process." "Yes, I will attend." "OK, let's get you signed up."

As I drove home, I began to think, what a relief, maybe I will be able to get some sleep over the next ten days. But what will I tell everyone? I dread calling my mother. She will be upset because Jeff has always been special to her. And of course, Anthony will be angry; he has never had much patience with his little brother. I can almost hear his response, "Mama, you are going to have to put your foot down with that boy."

I decided that there were several people with whom I wanted to talk when things settled down; especially, the high school football coaches. I had been upset with them since I learned that once, when I went out of town, Jeff threw a massive party for the football team in the faculty apartment where we were staying and that it got wild, and someone in the complex called the police. Several young men were taken to jail, and they called the coach. He had them released and suggested to Jeff that he not tell me about the incident. It was only after one of the faculty members from the college referred to the conflict that I became aware of what had happened. *Why would they not want me to know about the party?*

It seems as if driving the 30 miles home took forever. Getting into bed that evening was a welcomed relief.

"I will take tomorrow off and call everyone," I thought to myself. "I just can't deal with any questions tonight."

The next morning as I sipped a cup of coffee, I remember thinking, *"Oh, the peace, what a relief! I hope Jeff is doing OK. I'm sure that he is. I do believe that the move from his old school was a difficult adjustment for him. Maybe that was the reason he was drinking and doing other things? Well, here I go again, excusing him."* For every lie that he told, I had an excuse; for every confrontation we've had, I would invent an excuse. I had been covering up for him without knowing why. I remember with much shame the time we went to spend the weekend with a friend. When we got ready to leave, I woke him up and helped him get his shoes $50 fell out of his boot. I was stunned and asked where he had gotten the money? "Money, what are you talking about?" "You know what I'm talking about; did you take it from someone in this house? Go put it back!" I followed him to make sure that he put it back in the desk drawer.

On the way home, I tried to smooth it over by having another heart-to-heart talk with him about not taking from others. He was at least sixteen at the time. As I recall, I wish I had been more firm in my discussion and punishment. There was no punishment, just talk. Almost every time his brother would come home, there would be a significant blow-up, often because Jeff would take money or wear Anthony's clothes without permission. When caught and questioned, it would end up as our fault. "Oh, you love Anthony more than me. I'm the black sheep of the family." He began to withdraw from family gatherings.

Speaking of the family let me make those calls.

CHAPTER THREE

The White Elephant

I hesitated as I prepared for my first support group meeting. Although I wasn't supposed to be there until 6:00 p.m., I arrived early and sat in my car watching the door, hoping that I would not know anyone going into the meeting. As cars pulled into the parking lot, I took a quick inventory of those who got out and entered the building. I played a guessing game, *who were these people and who did they have in the facility?* The first couple to get out of their sleek black Buick was holding hands. They seemed to be quite upset. The woman's eyes were swollen and red. The man appeared to be disgruntled. Maybe they have a son who is seeking help. I sure hope that he hasn't given them as much trouble as I have experienced. *Wow! Who is that lady driving such a beautify Jaguar?* I could see money written all over her designer shoes and handbag. *Surely, she must be the class leader.* The next person to arrive appeared to be about my age; she too looked worried. She was alone and appeared to be Hispanic. *Oh well, enough of the guessing game. It's time to go in.*

When I walked into the meeting room, I walked with my head down, not wanting to make eye contact with anyone. I also headed for the back row. Soon, others arrived, and the small room grew even more modest. As if she planned the timing so that everyone would be there, a forty-something, plain-dressed woman appeared and introduced herself as the group leader. *There goes my theory about the lady driving the Jaguar.* "My name is Betty Riddle, and I will be your leader. Let me begin by congratulating each of you for seeking help." I clearly remembered thinking, *"I'm not the one needing help; it's Jeff, not me. If he would only get his act together, maybe, just maybe, I could enjoy life."*

Ms. Riddle continued to inform the group about her background in working with families who had lived with substance abusers. Afterward, she did what I hoped that she would not do. "Now that you know who I am, I would like for each of you to introduce yourself, giving only information that you are comfortable in sharing." Introductions took forever. Most everyone wanted to share his/her story, and some cried during their testimony. Others sobbed as they began to unfold their life history about a child or spouse. The most shocking story was that of a daughter whose seventy-year-old mother was getting treatment for being addicted to prescription drugs. As each story was shared, heads were nodding in agreement. On several occasions, people even said a few, "amen's." There was an instant bonding within the group. Also, though the characters may seem different, the stories were connected. We all have something in common.

Ms. Riddle stood and asked a question, "How do you get the white elephant out of your living room?" *What in the world is she talking about the white elephant?* "Have you ever heard about the white elephant? How much use do you have for a white elephant sitting in your living room? Well, some of you have had this elephant sitting there for years, and you don't know how to move it, and because you don't know how to move it, it's there every day. You have to feed it and clean up its mess. It's in the way. Everyone in the family has to work around this huge monster. It's in constant need of attention. On occasion, it will stomp its foot, and the whole house will shake, or it can make a sudden move, and everyone is disturbed by the noise. Heaven forbid if it wants attention. No one will be able to sleep until everyone is up and dealing with the elephant. Forget about making plans. No vacation, not even a night out to go to the movies. Who will take care of the elephant? What if something happens while you're away? You think that you're stuck, nowhere to run or hide, right?"

We all looked at each other as if to say, *"Get the damn elephant out of my house!"* Ms. Riddle continued by saying, "The elephant is dominating your life, but you think it's too big for you to handle – you can't get it out of your house. Well, it needs to move, and only you can move it. The elephant lives there because you have allowed it to live in your house. It has depended on you for survival. It needs to be free to roam and learn to survive on its own. You have been a codependent person for much too long . let it go." *Codependent . . . what does that mean?*

"Next week, we will talk about what it means to be codependent."

White elephant? Have I been living with this monster? You bet. The sucker has been living right there in my living room. It's so big I have not been able to move it. I can't go around it; I can't ignore it. I can't understand the needs of this monster. It's more than I can handle, I need help to understand the needs of my son!

CHAPTER FOUR

Partners in Crime

A s I drove home, I began to think about what Ms. Riddle said. *Codependent, what in the world does that have to do with me; what does it mean? I know what it means, but what does it really mean?*

Just as I predicted, my mother was upset that her favorite grandson was in a drug abuse treatment center. Anthony was even more confused than I ever remembered. "Mama, when are you going to turn that boy loose?" "He has done nothing but upset you since I've left home."I gave my usual excuses. I started by saying, "Well, you know that we just moved, and he has not been able to adjust, but I think that this will be the breaking point for him." *Yeah, right!*

One more call to make, I will need to let someone at the high school know. No, I don't think that I will call the principal. I'll go this afternoon and talk to the football coaches. I have a score to settle with them anyway. Oh, how happy they all were when we first moved to this hick town. I must admit that Jeff was a star athlete, even better than his brother. I will never forget the disappointment in his basketball coach's eyes when I told him that we were moving from Jacksonville, Florida to Georgia. I thought that he was going to cry. He said that it's only once in a lifetime that a coach has the opportunity to coach a young man with so much potential. He said that Jeff had extra large hands, and he had synchronized the ball methodically. I almost backed out; *maybe I should stay put, at least until Jeff graduates from high school. I can put my career on hold.*

Jeff was beyond angry, "Why do we have to move! I'll stay with a coach! I want to play football and basketball and will play the first string. I will not leave; you can go, but I'm not going!" After days of discussions, we came to a standoff, "Listen, young man, we will be leaving, and I suggest that you be ready to go."

At his new school, although his game was basketball, he tried out for the football team and instantly became a star. The coach even came over to the apartment to chat. "Ms. Dove, we sure are happy that you moved here. Jeffrey is a great player and also a fine young man." *Sure, you wait.* It didn't take very long before the addictive behavior began to rear its ugly head. He was in trouble at school, problem on the team, and issues in the community. The telephone calls started. *Why did I move? He was just fine; it's my fault.*

Now it's my time to visit the coach. "Yes, Coach, this is Ms. Dove. I want to come and talk with you and the other coaches about Jeffrey. Yes, I can be there by three. I'll meet you in the library." As I walked into the library, there sat four men, and not one of them was able to look me in the eye. I was angry. I wanted to say, "Please help me. You are all adult men; he will listen to you. You are the coaches; young men will listen to you." As I talked about the treatment center, and Jeffrey's problems, it appeared that all four knew much more than I knew. Now and then one of them would look up as if to say, "Lady, you don't know the half of it." Just when they thought that I had finished, I sprung my surprise on them. "Yes, and by the way, I know about the party." It felt good leaving on what I thought was a good note!

At the next support group meeting, Ms. Riddle entered the room with a confident smile and said, "Good evening." Most folks responded with a smile and nod. "How many of you have let the behavior of a person affect your life, and you respond by trying to control the personal behavior of the person?" Now, no one was nodding; no one was smiling. What I did see was a lot of plethora looks. "You are here because someone you love is in this facility, and that person is an addict. You have tried without success to control that person. You and that person are partners in crime. You, my dear friends, have been living a codependency life. The addict is addicted to drugs, alcohol, or prescription drugs, and you are addicted to trying to control the addict. The addict dominates your life because you allow him/her to do so. He/she is the white elephant that lives in your house. The addict depends on you for survival. You enable the behavior, and therefore you become partners in a cycle of addiction. At the beginning of the loved one's addiction, you tried to help by trying to control the addiction and the drug. But now your life is spiraling out of control. You aren't able to manage your life, nor the person who is addicted."

Now, I see heads nodding. I see people looking at each other in agreement. The Hispanic lady and I looked at each other with unspoken empathy. "Even today, some of you aren't sure that the person is an addict. You deny that there is a problem. There is a big problem. Drug addiction is a disease. It can be chronic, progressive, and it can be fatal, but it also can be treatable. The disease affects the mind as well as the physical body. There is no one to blame. No one plans to be an addict! Just as no one plans to get cancer or diabetes."

"The key to accepting that your loved one is ill is by working through the various stages to accept the disease and then rebuild a relationship that is healthy for everyone." Now people were sitting back in their seats, listening with attentive ears, my arms in a defense mode folded. *I'll hear, but I'm not buying it.* Moments later, I was not only listening, but I was also totally engaged, and especially after Ms. Riddle said that some studies have indicated that the disease can be genetic *unusual indeed.*

Someone asked her what the stages of codependence were? She thanked the person for the asking and said there are several stages, and they include: Denial, Anger, Bargaining, and Acceptance.

Denial: For most people in this stage, there is no addiction problem. Everyone may know that the person is an addict, but you may think that your son/daughter can't be using drugs; maybe because you live in a first-rate neighborhood and you already had that talk about not using drugs. There was no way that I wanted to admit that Jeff was using drugs, and if he was, it most certainly was not his fault, no way!

Ms. Riddle's second pointed:

Anger: The co-dependent person becomes so angry and needs to find someone to blame for the addiction. For me, it was the boy down the street, or maybe it was some of the older boys at schools. Everyone was to blame, of course, except Jeff. How many times did I cry out in anger, "What have I done to deserve this!" Ms. Riddle warned us that if we got stuck in the anger stage, our lives would forever be controlled by the abusers, mainly because we as co-dependents try to win over the drugs by controlling the environment, which is impossible. The more we try to control and fail, the angrier we become.

I came to realize that I was angry with Jeff most of the time. The rage that accelerated was almost uncontrollable. I think that most of the fury was due to embarrassment. I had worked so hard as a single parent to build a reputation as a good mother and provider. After all of the sacrifices that I made, didn't I attend all of their football and basketball games? Didn't I serve as den mother to their scout troops? I didn't just send them to church - we attended and participated as a family.

As Ms. Riddle talked about anger, I realized that not only was I angry with Jeff. I was mad with myself. I had failed, or so I thought.

In the next stage of codependency, which is Bargaining, you try to tell yourself that maybe it's not so bad. Perhaps if I can get the person out of this one situation, things will be better. After all, he/she promised to do better. How many times did I say, "Jeff, if you will improve your grades and not get in trouble for three weeks, I will..." How many times did I pray for divine intervention for just one more chance for him to get it right?

Also, Ms. Riddle talked about depression. I was the Queen of Depression. I didn't understand that I was powerless over his addiction. Ms. Riddle looked over the group and made a profound announcement: There is hope in the acceptance stage.

Acceptance doesn't mean approving drug use. It means that you still love the person, but you come to realize that you are powerless over the situation. You learn to accept the fact that as a codependent person, you need help for your survival. It is of paramount importance to learn to let go to make the addict learn from the consequences of his/her actions. After years of struggling as a codependent mother, it took me years to move from one stage to the other. On a scale of 1-10 of codependency, I considered myself to be a 10+.

The following week our group discussion focused on addiction and substance abuse. As I sat waiting on Ms. Riddle, I began to reflect on my introduction to alcohol. The session on addiction and substance abuse was one of the most educational sessions I attended. I attribute this to two factors: one the subject matter was new information, and secondly, I needed to know what was causing my son so much pain.

I grew up in a very rural southern town and drug use was not part of my culture. I had never heard the terms of marijuana or cocaine until I was a young adult and moved to the city. I never knew anyone who had used drugs in my circle of friends. However, I was very much aware of alcohol abuse. Several men in my family drank too much, including my father. As a teen, I had a special friend, and she and I would occasionally take a beer and several cigarettes from our parents and go off into the woods or outhouse to pretend that we were adults by smoking and sharing a beer. On several occasions, one of our siblings threatened to tell our parents. Cheap beer was the drink of choice for most of my peers, and this was only on special occasions, after winning a significant football game or when we were able to sneak a beer from our parents.

Ms. Riddle started by saying that most families have been affected by substance abuse and addiction, and that substance abuse is a severe problem. At this point, all eyes were on Ms. Riddle. She went on to say that substance abuse usually leads to addictions that influence compulsive behavior, too much alcohol, drugs, prescription medicine, sex, gambling, food, nicotine, and even shopping!

She continued by saying some people believe that marijuana is harmless, although the effects may vary depending on the person. It can be very counterproductive, as well as a depressant.

For young people, the use of marijuana can lead to social and emotional problems that can affect a person's relationship with families and friends. The person may do or say things that they would typically not do. Teenage males will mainly take a risk, which may put them in danger; for example, a vehicle may become a lethal weapon, and speeding while using the drug becomes the norm. Marijuana almost always makes people less motivated. It changes how the user thinks or feels, and learning is severely affected. Also, perception, thinking memory, and even emotions may be affected. It's safe to say that failure in school becomes the norm. She said that the high school graduation rate is very low for heavy users of marijuana.

Her next statement was shocking, "Studies indicate that heavy alcohol and marijuana use affects the developing brain in adolescents who may develop learning and memory impairment." Yet another shocker came when she announced that the age in which the person began to use drugs or alcohol is the maturity age of the person, regardless of the chronological age. It is due in part to the number of brain cells that are damaged. Also, it may take years for the brain to repair itself even after a person has stopped using alcohol or drugs. In most cases, the brain is never fully restored.

I raised my hand, "Yes, Ms. Dove?" "Please tell us about cocaine." Well, cocaine is very addictive. For some people, the addiction comes very quickly; sometimes as early as the first use depending on the amount used and the purity of the cocaine. It is a stimulant because it speeds up the nervous system, and, in some cases, it can cause a heart attack, which could lead to death. It can damage the brain, heart, and other organs.

Like other drugs, cocaine will cause the "White Elephant" to steal, lie, and participate in other self-destructive behavior. Someone asked, "Why do you think people young and old use drugs?" Ms. Riddle replied, "For many reasons. In my line of work, I've heard many stories." She said the most common answer from teens was to "fit in" with their friends. Others say they are curious, but most of them believe that they will not become addicted.

As she turned to face the group, she asked, "How many of you know that heroin belongs to a group called Opiates? What are Opiates? They are strong pain-killers and are depressants that slow down the nervous system. Heroin usually comes in a powder form that can be injected, snorted, or smoked. If used long enough, it can damage the veins, heart, and lungs. People who share needles and syringes may be at risk for contracting diseases."

A father in the group said, "My son told his mother and me that he had used Ecstasy. We read that it speeds up the nervous system. What more can you tell us?" "Ms. Riddle responded well, Ecstasy is often mixed with a variety of drugs and can be dangerous if taken in combination with other medications. Ecstasy can lead to several psychological and physical problems. Other effects can include loss of appetite, insomnia, or depression.

"Folks," declared Ms. Riddle, "Let's not forget that alcohol, although legal, can become just as addictive as illegal drugs. The fact is that more and more teenagers drink alcohol, which is becoming a serious problem affecting our youth. Some are young as elementary and junior high age students. Some have a dual addiction, drugs, and alcohol." Someone from the back of the room shouted, "Why?"

Ms. Riddle paused for a moment as if to be careful to choose the right words. "We now know that addiction is a disease. It's more than not having enough 'will power.' Scientists now believe that there is a genetic link that may cause addictive behavior. Some think that it can be inherited." Ms. Riddle paused as she looked toward the ceiling. "Let me tell you about my son, who is fourteen years old. His father and I are divorced. His father is an alcoholic; his grandfather is an alcoholic; his uncles are alcoholics; I firmly believe that a genetic link causes the generational repeat of alcoholism. I have begun to talk with my son about the dangers of addiction. I told him that, "based on my research, he should never take one sip of alcohol because of the danger of him becoming addicted."I now believe that education is the best weapon for children of addictive parents and more research should continue on the biological causes of addiction

Another person asked what some signs or symptoms of alcoholism or drug addiction are. How will you know if your son or daughter is drinking or using drugs? "Good question!" said Ms. Riddle. Some of the common signs may include:

- Changes in school work and attendance; discipline problems
- Outbreaks of temper; easy to become upset
- Sunglasses inappropriately used
- Stealing small amounts of things and money
- Cannot make eye contact
- Attention span is short
- Eating binges, especially sweets
- Loss of weight
- Change in personality; becomes mean
- Clothes are unkempt
- Red eyes
- Weird friends
- Avoiding family gatherings
- Slurred speech
- Driving slowly
- A dazed look
- Late sleeping
- Not motivated
- Difficulty focusing

CHAPTER FIVE

Tough Love

A re you at your wits end? Do you find yourself giving in when you should be standing your ground? Do you have a pattern of weaknesses? Does your child run the family unit? Does your child cause confusion, frustration, and stress in your life? Do you allow your child to make mistakes? Are you firm? Do you make decisions with your heart rather than your head? Are you fearful of your teenager?

These questions were posted on the board when we gathered for our group session. In bold letters at the top were two words, "Tough Love."

As Mrs. Riddle began the discussion on tough love, it was as if she was writing the script, especially for me. I also got the impression that everyone in the room felt the same. People were sitting at attention, holding on to each word.

She began by affirming that tough love is about being firm and putting your foot down. It's about being assertive . . . "no means no."

She maintained that tough love should also include loving our loved ones unconditionally. However, we do not have to approve or support what they are doing by being an enabler.

In our discussion, she gave a litany about tough love.

Tough love is excruciating and stressful. However, I have learned that it's probably one of the best techniques for any teenager, not just those who are abusing drugs and alcohol.

Parents should be parents and not buddies with their children. I believe that teenagers want boundaries. The reason I say this is because I remember when I was about sixteen years old, I was invited by friends to attend a party that was being given by someone older than my usual crowd. I had mixed feelings about going, I didn't want to go, but I was too "chicken" to say no. I was betting on my mother saying "no" because I was supposed to be grounded for breaking my curfew the week before. I had stayed out past my curfew. When I asked her, her response was, "Aren't you on restriction?" I quickly replied, "Yes!" My mother took a long suspicious look as if to say no way. To my surprise, she said yes! I remember thinking why didn't she stick to her "guns." Although my mother was a kind-hearted and gentlewoman; she was not one to stand her ground when it came to tough love, in the end, she would give in. Lucky for her, my siblings and I were somewhat functional teens, and besides, my father was the author of the "Just Say No" slogan.

Ms. Riddle continued pressing forward with the tough love theme. She reminded the group that young people who are involved in addictive behavior patterns tend to be immature and irresponsible. It is the responsibility of the parent to make rational decisions.

On the drive home that night, I began to reflect on Ms. Riddle's comment about how addictive people tend to be immature and irresponsible. Immediately I thought of the incidence that Jeff was involved in several months earlier. His high school baseball team was having a home game. There was no admissions charge. However, Jeff and several of his friends decided to stand at the gate and charge a $2.00 fee. Yes, they were caught! And why not? They were collecting from everyone, including the high school principal! I developed my own ten commandments.

TEN COMMANDMENTS OF TOUGH LOVE

1. *Thou shall ask God to give you the will power to exercise tough love*
2. *Thou shall know the difference between letting someone abuse you and use you*
3. *Thou shall not harm a child or loved one in a fit of anger or rage*
4. *Thou shall write the word "no" on thy forehead with irremovable paint finish*

5. *Thou shall be strong and firm when dealing with dysfunctional teens and anyone else*

6. *Thou shall make the choice to love thyself by setting boundaries, and not serving as a doormat for other people*

7. *Thou shall understand that those involved in self-destructive behavior have no reason to change if they do not ever suffer major consequences for their behavior*

8. *Thou shall promise to seek help for self to grow and accept the things that you cannot change*

9. *Thou shall know and realize when enough is enough!*

10. *Thou shall thank God for your recovery steps and go on a much needed vacation to celebrate "tough love" --- Free at last, Thank God Almighty, Free at last*

CHAPTER SIX

The Red Bandanna

As soon as Jeff was allowed to have visitors, my mother called and said that she would be coming to visit Jeff. After she arrived at my home, we drove up for a visit. As we waited for him to come out, we sat in the lobby. As we entered the lobby, I was surprised to see the Hispanic mother sitting in the lobby. She and I began to talk, and our stories were the same. Jeff and her son were about the same age. As we continued to chat, both boys came out about the same time. Jeff was all smiles and had a red bandanna tied around his head. He sure looked good in red; I was surprised as to how great he looked. Jeff looked peaceful and well-rested. He first ran to his grandmother and gave her a big hug. As usual, our greeting was standoffish; however, I was happy to see him. We chatted for a few minutes before signing him out.

We decide to go downtown. There was a festival, and the main street was blocked off. There was music, and people selling home craft items. My mom and I took in the sites, and Jeff appeared to be enjoying the freedom of being outdoors. Later, we had lunch. Jeff gave a very brief account of his experiences in the treatment center, and I didn't push the issue. On the way back, he talked with his grandmother, and as always, they were able to have a genuine conversation. When we arrived at the Center and were preparing to say our good-byes, as I looked at him, I saw a seventeen-year-old young man who was fighting back the tears. I saw a young man that I didn't know yet whom I had given birth. I wanted to reach out and give him a big hug and tell him how much I loved him. But just as I was getting ready to reach out, he turned and said goodbye as he walked away. My mother was excited about the visit and was hopeful that this time he would make a turn-around. I must admit that I, too, was optimistic.

On Wednesday, after our visit, one of the group counselors from the treatment center called. *Why is he calling - did something happened? What now?* "Ms. Dove, we gave Jeffrey a urine test when he got back on Saturday, and he did not pass it." "What do you mean? He was with us the entire time, never out of my sight." "Well, don't worry about it, sometimes these tests will come back negative, and there is another explanation. We will retest him." To this day, I don't know what happened. I never asked.

CHAPTER SEVEN

A Bittersweet Journey

Jeff's senior year should have been full of activities and celebrations that he would later look back on with pride and joy, but as it turned out, it was a bittersweet final year of high school. He had a sweet athletic year and bittersweet academic year. As an educator, I have always been against so much focus on a student's athletic ability and not enough attention paid to the academic achievement of the athlete, especially African-American males.

During Jeff's senior year, I served as the co-secretary of the high school Touchdown Club. At one of our meetings, I suggested that we get students from the college to tutor the football players. After talking with the coaching staff, I cannot adequately express my disappointment at their lack of response to my suggestion. Initially, none of them spoke in favor of the idea. They all looked at me as if I had said something that they did not comprehend. Finally, the head coach said, "When would the boys find the time to work with a tutor?" I recall saying, "These young men will do whatever you want them to do. You tell them when and where and they will show up." The other secretary spoke up and said, "I think it is a great idea! also." She added that forty-five minutes before school started could work if parents would agree to bring the players in early. The head coach jumped in and said, "But you will need to sell the idea to the "boys" and their parents!"

I agreed to send a letter to all the parents and recruit students from the college to tutor the students. Several weeks later, we were ready for our first session. The first meeting was an orientation meeting; notices went to parents, coaches, and students. Jeff and I were the first to arrive, and about three minutes later, another student came in by himself. That was the group, the three of us! The other young man turned out to be an "A" student. The three of us met for about two to three weeks, and in all that time, no one else showed up. I never did hear any more from the coaching staff about the tutoring sessions.

After being discharged from the rehabilitation center, I was hopeful that things would turn around. When Jeff returned to school, I had a meeting with his teachers. They informed me that there wasn't much hope that Jeff would be able to graduate with his class. He had fallen behind in at least two categories; his teachers indicated that he had missed too much work to catch-up, and because of this, he would not receive enough high school credits to graduate. When I talked with him about the possibility of him not graduating, I could see the disappointment in his eyes and the emotional pain in his face. Although he came across as a strong and independent young man, what I had learned about substance abusers lead me to believe that even he knew that he was in over his head and was suffering from low self-esteem.

Things would have been different, if not for the substance. My family always believed that he was a star athlete, both in football and basketball, and would receive a college athletic scholarship. He received an All-Middle Georgia Athletic Award for his athletic achievement. His senior year was his best as a star athlete, week after week, he would be highlighted in the area newspaper sports section.

Baldwin seniors go out in style

Braves rout Northeast in finale, 31-8

By Don Carswell
Staff writer

Baldwin High said goodbye to one of its best graduating classes in the last few years with a season-ending 31-8 win over Northeast-Macon at homecoming Friday night.

The seniors accounted for all of the Braves' points as Baldwin dominated the Raiders from the opening kickoff.

Baldwin head coach Bill Boyd, although unhappy about a 6-4 season, was pleased to his seniors go out on a winning note.

"It's good any time that you win the last ball game, and that was

number nine in a row as far as homecoming is concerned," said Boyd, whose team 3-4 in the Georgia High School Association Region AAAA. "I would have liked to have seen the boys go out with a shutout because that's the one way the defensive boys can win.

"They wanted to go out big time and they did go out big time. There a good group of kids and I hate to see them go. I wish we had them again next year. We'd find a way to win those ballgames.

"They were very instrumental winning a region crown last year sure as heck would have been nice go out in a blaze of glory and getting after that region crown again."

After stopping Northeast on it, first possession, the Braves' Henry Hill, a senior defensive back, returned a punt 44 yards to the Raider 10. David Hill scored on Baldwin's first play from scrimmage on a sweep around right end.

Hill, who rushed for 113 yards on eight carries, set a new Baldwin record with 1,157 yards, breaking Kenny Thomas' old record of 1,057 set in 1984.

The Braves, who held Northeast to one first down in the first half, shut down Northeast again to set up another quick touchdown.

Senior wide receiver Jeff Dove made a great one-handed catch for 53 yards down to the Northeast eight-yard line. Senior fullback Ray Reynolds then took it in on a run right up the middle.

Senior kicker Donald Evans made it 17-0 when he kicked a 39-yard field goal early in the second quarter.

Baldwin added two more touchdowns in the second half when senior quarterback Carlos Miller went up the middle for a 16-yard scoring punt. Miller, who rushed for 39 yards in the game, completed nine of

HOMECOMING page 19

45

;oyd says Braves /ant second game gainst Southwest

Don Carswell
ff writer

To his own regret, Baldwin High head coach Bill Boyd ned out to be a prophet.

In an interview last Wednesday, Boyd had said that if Southwest Patriots came in and played error free tball, his team would be in trouble.

The Patriots had only one turnover in Friday's game, ding to a 31-30 upset of the Braves in the Region 4-AA opener for each team.

That one fumble was offset by a Baldwin fumble, the ly other turnover of the night. Both fumbles led to ahdowns for the opposing teams.

The Braves were hurt by penalties throughout the me. A key penalty, that eventually led to the Baldwin 'nover, was pass interference play called against Bald-n. When the flag was thrown, four Baldwin defenders re around the Southwest receiver.

Baldwin just missed winning the game at the end. On a final play of the game Carlos Miller threw a pass that unded off the hands of a Southwest defender into the nds of running back David Hill. Hill, who had earlier ored on a 73-yard reception, was knocked out at the uthwest 20 to end the game.

Southwest was hit with a roughing the passer penalty keep Baldwin's hopes alive. Unfortunately for the aves, high school rules say that roughing the passer is t a dead ball foul. In college and in the NFL, it is a ad ball foul and is added to the end of the play.

So rather than having the ball at the Southwest 10, here a field goal would win the game, Baldwin had to ke the ball at the 50. By taking the play, the game uld be over. Miller's long pass on the next play was itted away to end the game.

Miller was one of a few bright spots in the loss.

The senior quarterback had one of his best games, impleting 12-of-18 passes for 217 yards and four scores.

"Well, he had an outstanding game," said Boyd. "I'd ve to compliment him. The kid did a super job."

Boyd felt that the inconsistency of his team's defense d to the final outcome. He pointed to a youthful squad one of the reasons for the inconsistency.

SAM WALTON/ Staff Photographer

Jeff Dove is all smiles after touchdown

"We played well at times. We didn't play well enough or long enough.

"We've got eight kids coming back, so there's a lot of inexperience there. Hopefully we can survive the storm, come on this next week and be a little more consistent."

The obvious problem for Baldwin was a versatile offense on the other side of the ball. Southwest picked up 18 first downs while using a very balanced attack.

The Patriots picked up 173 yards passing and 174 yards rushing. Sophomore quarterback Joe Dupree led the way, throwing for 173 yards. Junior wide receiver Darren Willis haunted the Baldwin secondary, catching eight passes for 141 yards.

"No. 7 (Willis) absolutely blew past us. We had kids in position for interceptions and Dupree laid the ball exact-ly where he had to leave it. The guys (Southwest) did the job they had to do."

Boyd, a man who hates to lose, even at "tiddlywinks", is looking for a chance to face Southwest head coach, and good friend, Edgar Hatcher again.

"It's nothing revengeful, Edgar's a nice guy. But he beat me. I hope I get to face that rascal again, because I'm going to beat him."

Later, he began to receive letters from colleges all over the country. They all wanted to congratulate Jeff on his athletic achievement and to inform him of their athletic program. In some cases, we received letters from "Booster Club" members sharing information about their association with the school and its exceptional athletic program. However, at the end of the school year, there was no graduation and no scholarship.

Jeff received letters from as far away as California, Indiana, Kentucky, Tennessee, and Missouri.

CHAPTER EIGHT

Fighting My Demons

Five years earlier, about the same time that I began to notice a change in Jeff, there was also something that was taking place in my life that was eating at the very core of my soul! One morning as I prepared for work, as usual, I was listening to the television. As I rushed around, I could hear the voices on the early morning religious talk show. I had begun to listen to this particular program for about six months. Although I wasn't very fond of the host, something said caught my attention. I remember coming back into the room when I heard the host state, "If you do not know Jesus Christ as your personal Lord and Savior, pray the sinner's prayer with me." Although I had attended church most of my life and considered myself a Christian, that morning, I stopped and prayed. "Dear Lord, I accept your son Jesus as Lord and Savior and want to turn my life around." On my way to work, as I drove toward the expressway, I began to have a strange feeling in the pit of my stomach. It felt empty or a black hole.

That morning was the beginning of a journey that almost caused me to throw in the towel of life. In the next two years of my experience, I lived in two different worlds divided between the worlds of light and darkness – good and evil.

That morning, the moment I accepted Jesus Christ as my Lord and Savior, Satan waged an all-out attack. The sick feeling of emptiness in the pit of my stomach was there seven days a week, twenty-four hours a day.

Although I wasn't sure what it was, I had a feeling that it had something to do with my accepting Jesus Christ as my Lord and Savior.

I didn't know who to talk to; even if I did, how I could explain what was happening to me. It got to the point where I did not want to get up in the mornings because as soon as my eyes opened, the attack would start. Day after day, each day, I had to force myself to go to work and even to eat. What had I done to experience such a wilderness experience?

I began to read the Bible, and although I had always attended church, I had no clue about the order and structure of the Christian Canon. I began to pray. Nothing changed.

Three months into the inner warfare, I began searching the yellow pages to find a Christian counselor.

In bold print on about a half-page of advertisement were the words: Christian Counseling Group. I put the book down and began to talk myself out of making an appointment. *Who would believe me? How could I explain what I was feeling?* The pain was so profound, but what did I have to lose? I made the call.

My appointment was for 10:00 a.m. on a Friday. After arriving at the office, the war began to intensify. I almost got up to leave when the counselor came out to get me; she was wearing a black suit with a white blouse. She looked the part of a clean-cut Christian counselor. "Ms. Dove, please come in. How did you find us? Did someone refer you?" I explained that I searched the Yellow Pages. As we talked, I began to speak in a roundabout way about what I was feeling. The counselor finally asked, "Who or what do you think is causing these thoughts?" I could not respond. She responded, "Do you think it's Satan?" The flood gates opened, and I cried tears of relief. Finally, someone knew what I was experiencing.

I don't remember much more about that day, but I do know that the attacks did not stop. Finally, several months later, I decided to stay home from work. And lock myself within my home and pray.

On September 19, 1980, after praying and fasting, around 2:30 p.m., I began to feel a strange warm feeling over my body. I began to lift my hands toward heaven, praising God! There was a joy that I had never experienced before, a peace that was beyond my comprehension.

CHAPTER NINE

A Journey to the Promise Land

During Jeff's senior year, I applied for jobs at several colleges closer to the Atlanta area. One of the reasons I wanted to move closer to Atlanta was because I was dating someone who was living in Atlanta, and we were talking about getting married. We wanted to wait until after Jeff had finished high school and gone away to college. I applied to a two-year institution and received an offer. In July, we moved to Oakwood, Georgia.

By this time, I had begun to step up my "tough love" stance. The elephant was moving closer to the exit door. I was no longer willing to allow Jeff to dictate my life. I decided that I would set a time limit for him to get a high school diploma and to work on a plan to transition from my house to his house. My suggestion was for him to get a GED. However, my advice was not received very well. He wanted to go to an area high school and finish the two classes that he needed to graduate. I was against him attending a high school in the city because I was afraid that history would repeat itself. I was worried that he would get involved with drugs and alcohol, and I would have to deal with it once again. I was ready to move on with my life. When we sat down and discussed his options for getting his diploma, I finally agreed to give him one semester to finish his course work. I made it clear that after that semester, he should have a plan for the future.

The high school that he selected was out of the school district, where I had gotten an apartment. For him to enroll, I had to pay an out-of-district fee.

The other challenge was transportation for him to get to school. I decided to buy him a used car because I did not want to take and pick him up from school. In hindsight, I now realize that buying him a car was a big, big mistake. He now had the freedom to explore uncharted territory in new surroundings.

One morning around 1:00 a.m. there was a loud bang, bang on the door. Peeking through the peek hole, I saw a flashlight pointed to the door; it was the police. *What now?* Standing next to the policeman was Jeff. "Ms. Dove, I found your son in a ditch with two flat tires, "the policeman said. The policeman continued to move his lips, but I could not hear a word that he was saying;

my brain froze. I was brought back to reality when someone was shouting, "Ms. Dove, are you okay?" "Yes, I'm okay. Yes, thanks, officer." After the officer left, Jeff came through the door, and I opened my mouth to say something but nothing would come out. A small voice said, "go to bed!" I was happy to obey the command. I turned and went upstairs, got into bed, and pulled the covers over my head.

Several weeks later, I went to the mailbox to pick up my mail, which was the day for me to receive a dependent allotment check that I received each month from Social Security. To my surprise, there was no check. The next day, I met the mailman and asked about my mail from the day before. He said, "Oh, yes, yesterday a tall young man, who said he was your son, picked up your mail. Immediately I knew that I would never get to cash that check.

I didn't see Jeff for two days. When he finally came to the apartment, I told him that I knew that he had gotten the check. His response was, "Yes, but it's for me from my dead daddy." "The check even says for Jeffrey Dove."

I can remember thinking, "This is it!" I asked him to pack his bags and leave my apartment. To my surprise, he said, "No, I don't have anywhere to go." I picked up the telephone and called the police. When the officer arrived, he listened as I told him the story, and after I finished, he said, "Okay young man, let's go." Jeff said, "What do you mean; I'm in high school." The officer said, "You are seventeen, and your mother has a right to ask you to leave her apartment – now go pack a bag, and I will drive you to where ever you want to go." He left sitting in the back of a patrol car.

Several days later, the phone rang. "Mama, I'm going to check myself into a county rehab center for ten days." "Okay, take care of yourself," I replied.

After he got out of rehab, he called and said that he had been sleeping on a park bench for several days and wanted to come home to talk with me. As we sat talking, I knew that most of what he was saying was a "con." "Tell her what she wants to hear."

By this time, Lee and I had decided to get married. I wanted to resolve the issue with Jeff finishing high school. While he was in rehab, I had obtained information about the military and the GED exam. There would be no more going to high school or negotiations; it was, sign up for the army or else! That Monday morning, I took him to the military recruiter's office. The process did not take long; within a month, he had received a GED and was on his way to Oklahoma for basic training.

Lee and I married about two weeks before Jeff left for boot camp. In that short time, things were tense at home. We had bought a new house, and trying to mesh three different people under one roof was not going well. I began to count the days before Jeff would leave. My baby boy left home. I waited for this moment for eighteen years! Now I could relax and enjoy my new life, a new beginning – marriage, a job, and freedom from parenthood. I remember thinking, "the elephant has finally moved." The journey to the Promised Land was no comfortable journey, but we made it!

After receiving manna from heaven, to my surprise, about two weeks after Jeff left for basic training, I was rearranging some furniture in my dining room, and I began to cry. I thought to myself, it sure feels strange not having any kids to take care of, no yelling, no fighting – so why are you crying? I later concluded that I was experiencing the "empty nest syndrome." It's strange how our bodies react to life. I had finally reached the Promised Land yet, not satisfied with the results.

Later, Lee and I began to adjust to married life. Jeff would call from boot camp, and it appeared that he was adjusting to military life. Lee and I even drove out to Oklahoma for his graduation from "boot camp." We stayed the weekend, and for the first time in a long time, we laughed and had fun like old times.

You're in the Army Now!

CHAPTER TEN

Not Me, Lord!

All during this time of crossing the wilderness with Jeffrey, I continued to have a "Jacob" experience. I was in a constant battle with an angel of God. There was this ever-present spirit within me almost from the day that I prayed and accepted Jesus Christ as my Lord and Savior. The message was clear that I was being "called" to ordained ministry.

By no means did I hear a voice from a burning bush directing me to go and proclaim the gospel. I just knew. Although my inner "spirit" convinced me of my calling, my human self was telling me that there was no way that God would call me, a woman, to preach the gospel. Clearly, I remember on one occasion while driving on the interstate, when I became acutely aware of a stirring presence within my being. I became annoyed and cried out, "not me leave me alone!" "I don't want to preach," and then I added, "Why don't you call Jeff to preach; he is the one who needs to clean up his act. He is the one who needs to change his life for the better?

The comeback answer that I received shocked me. I got off at the next exit and parked the car. The response: "I know all about Jeff and you. I'm calling both of you to proclaim the gospel."

I was stunned and begun to laugh. I think I said something to the effect, "God, if you can turn Jeff around to preach the gospel, I will know that you are who you say "you are." After that announcement, I had so many questions. How could I become a preacher? Who would believe me if I told them that I felt a need to pursue ministry? And now you say Jeff will also preach the gospel? Surely I must be getting the wrong messages.

As I pondered the "call" to ordained ministry, there was another mountain that I needed to climb. How could I tell Lee my thoughts about preaching? Although he was a kind man, he was also from the "old school" of religious doctrine that forbade women to preach. Even though I don't think that at the time he realized it, he was very much grounded in his Baptist roots, which said that men are the head of the house and the church. How could I tell him that I was struggling with a need to preach?

As a couple, we had not identified a place of worship, but after settling down in our marriage, Lee and I began to attend a Baptist church in our community. On occasion, I continued to worship at a United Methodist Church in

Atlanta. Soon, Lee began to feel at home worshipping in his Baptist roots, but I wasn't drawn spiritually to the church. I was drawn to the Methodist church, my Christian roots. My maternal side of the family was Methodists. Maybe I was comfortable with the Methodist Church because there was a female associate pastor at the church I was attending, and I loved to hear her pray. At the time, I could see myself through her. Without her knowing it, she was my role model.

I later became a member of the United Methodist Church, and Lee became a member of the Baptist church.

Things came to a head with the wrestling angel and me one Friday morning. I was at home, and it was pouring down rain outside. As I looked out the window, I began to cry and pray. My prayer was simple, "Lord, I yield, if you are calling me to ordained ministry, open the doors that I need to go through, and I promise you that I will do whatever it is that you would have me to do." At that very moment, I was at peace, and later that day, I made an appointment to talk with my pastor about my call.

Out of respect for Lee, I knew that I would have to talk with him before meeting with the pastor. To my surprise, after telling him my story, he looked me directly in the eyes and said, "Who am I to say who God calls to proclaim the Gospel?"

On the day of my appointment to meet with the Pastor, I began to doubt myself I didn't know if he would believe my story.

As I sat outside his office, I began to panic. I remember saying, "You are going to make a fool of yourself." The pastor's office door opened and out walked this tall guy with a deep voice that sounded like thunder. "Good morning my sister, come on in and have a seat." As he sat at his desk looking at me, I finally said, "I don't know where to begin." He said, "Why don't you begin at the beginning. " Halfway through my story, I began to cry. When I finished my story, this giant of a man came over and put his arm around my shoulder and said, "Who told you my story? Your story sounds like my story." Then he added, "God always wins!"I was on cloud nine, he believed me. Soon after that, the church board approved me to become a candidate for ordained ministry.

To this day, I can't clearly explain how I arrived at Emory University – Candler School of Theology. Although it was a three-year program of study to receive a Master's of Divinity Degree, it took me four years to complete the degree, because I continued to work full-time. I continually worked, attending school, preparing for classes, writing papers, assisting in the church as a student pastor, and being a wife. Although I was consumed with busy work, I was at peace with my decision to attend seminary. Often I remark that the most personal and profound educational growth for me came from attending seminary. Questions raised during the seminary educational journey allowed me to understand and appreciate the thoughts and ideas of others from an all-inclusive religious perspective. When introduced to the theological concept of "free will," I began to understand human's relationship with a supreme being.

It was at Candler that I learned about contributions women made to the Christian church. To my surprise, as early as 1801, Dorothy Ripley, a Christian Methodist missionary, came to America and met with President Thomas Jefferson concerning the slave controversy in America. It was during my studies on the impact of women on Christianity I became aware of the history of the Salvation Army. Like most Americans, I understood the Salvation Army to be a non-profit organization that reached out to all people in times of distress. However, it's much more; it's a Christian church with a heart for outreach. Catherine Booth was a co-founder.

In 1891, the Wesleyan Methodist Church voted to allow women to be ordained, and in 1980, Marjorie Matthews became the first woman elected bishop. In 1984 Leontine T. C. Kelly became the first black female bishop of the United Methodist Church.

For me, this information confirmed that God's power works in mysterious ways.

CHAPTER ELEVEN

Born a Free Spirit

Although I was busy trying to keep up with my involvement in a multitude of tasks, I had begun to feel some sense of relief. Jeff was in California, hopefully doing okay. Seminary was a dream comes true, and Lee and I were finally settling into our marriage. However, there continued to be a part of me that kept me from fully embracing life. The one thing that I longed for was a lasting peace that "surpasses all human understanding."

It was as if I was waiting for the bad news. The telephone would ring, and I would jump. Believe it or not, a part of me envied Jeff; he had a "free spirit. When I use the term free spirit, I'm not solely speaking of behavior due to addiction. Jeff was born with a need to be free. As a baby, he would resist structured play or activities. The happiest playtime for him was playing alone, to explore the environment. He also developed a compassion for others, especially those who he felt were mistreated, or the underdog. My mother loved to tell the story about the time she was giving her companion the third degree, and Jeff came and sat on her lap and said, "Grandma, please don't fuss at Boatwright, leave him alone!" She later confessed that she had gone overboard, and a little boy put her to shame.

Throughout the years, Jeff's philosophy had been - take each day at a time, money is to spend, especially someone else's money, enjoy life, let tomorrow take care of itself, and why save for a rainy day – there may not be another day.

Taking risks got him excited. He sought opportunities for adventure. A prime example of this came in the form of him driving from Georgia to California by himself at age 18.

Shortly after "basic training," he called to say that he wanted to come home and get his Jeep.

"Do you mean driving back to California by yourself?"

I was against it. Lee stepped up as the voice of reason.

"He is no longer a little boy, give him a chance."

A month later, as he pulled out of the driveway of our home, map in hand, on his way out west, I felt a surge of jealousy. There goes a "free spirit." Later, Lee informed me that he had asked Jeff to call in every day, the reason being, "so your mother will not worry."

About two days into the trip, the phone rang.

"Hello, you have a collect call from Jeffrey Dove."

"Yes, I will accept the call."

"Mama, can you wire me some money?"

"Money For what?"

"Well, I'm out of money, and I had a flat tire."

I had no idea how much money he had when he left Georgia; I just assumed that he had enough for the trip. My thoughts were interrupted when he said, "I slept in the car at a rest area last night . . . um, um ."

Mom and Dad. I was in my first trimester of pregnancy with Jeff.

After receiving the money, he called and informed me that he had gotten a hotel room, and in his words, "I'm in bed, watching TV, drinking a "cold one" and chilling. *"I can't believe that the boy would take my money and buy beer!"* I looked toward heaven and said, "God, you've got your work cut out for you. Good luck."

"You have a collect call from Jeffrey Dove."

"Yes."

"Guess where I am? I'm in California riding on the beach, and it is beautiful. The water is so clear."

I could finally breathe a sigh of relief. The excitement in his voice said it all, "I'm free!"

CHAPTER TWELVE

Kevin

There was another young man in my life that was born with a free spirit. Even though he was not my biological son, I loved him as a son. His mother and I are "very best friends." We both graduated from the same college and are sorority sisters. I watched her two children grow up, and to them, I was Auntie Theresa. Her son, Kevin, was a very articulate and handsome young man. At an early age, he was also an excellent football player and a well-mannered young man. He and his sister Nicole attended private school until around the eighth or ninth grade. I remember attending high school football games. In addition to being a great athlete, he was very popular in and out of school. The girls loved him!

After graduating high school, he went off to a well-established university. He became a theater major. Almost immediately, his mother became concerned that he was drinking too much. On one occasion, she commented that she was worried about the amount of beer and alcohol that he was drinking during spring break. After his first year in college, I, too, began to notice a significant change in Kevin's personality. He was no longer the happy-go-lucky young man that I knew. Even his behavior changed towards his mother; because she questioned his drinking and change in behavior. He became very defensive. When he returned to college the second year, his parents continued to see signs of substance abuse. His grades began to fall, as he was not as focused academically. After learning that he was not attending class, they called him for an explanation. Of course, he convinced them that he was indeed going to class. They later learned about his suspension from the university for failure to keep on track academically. His father and grandfather rented a U-Haul, and went to Tallahassee, packed him up, and brought him home. Things began to go downhill for Kevin. He even had several minor encounters with the law.

On March 03, 1996, I was on my way out the door when the phone rang. It was a mutual friend of Pat, Kevin's mom. Immediately I knew something was wrong. She said I have some bad news. Kevin is dead. I remember screaming on the phone, and Lee came and asked, "What's wrong?" I was not able to answer. He took the phone and began to get all of the details. We immediately canceled our plans for the day and drove to Jacksonville, Florida, to be with my friend and her family.

Kevin's death was due in part to his association with drugs and alcohol. An older brother and sister killed him. They said that he had stolen money from them. I remember thinking; another promising young man's life was interrupted by the hands of older corrupt individuals. I had a flashback about the Corvette driver. We later learned that the brother and sister had been in trouble with the law due to illegal drug activity.

CHAPTER THIRTEEN

Be Careful of Judgment

Jeff's tenure in the Army was not without adversary. His goal was to train in the elite squad as an airborne parachutist. However, a military background check revealed his past, and he was not accepted for the training because of his drug rehab stay. Once again, he was disappointed with his past. When he called home, I heard that familiar voice of disappointment, "I did not make the airborne team."

After basic training, he transferred to California.

My mother always wanted to take an airplane trip out west. Like most women her age, she had never been on an airplane. What better opportunity for me to fulfill her dream than to take her to California to visit her grandson.

Our trip would be a Mother's Day get-a-way. Although I had been to California on several occasions, I was excited that I would be the child who would take my mother to California. At the time, I did not realize how wise and courageous my mother was. She had another motive for wanting to go to California. In addition to wanting to explore the adventures of the west, she also wanted to give moral support to Jeff.

Even though I had some concerns that my mother would become fearful during the flight, to my amazement, she sat next to the window and gazed out with much delight, not even a hint of fear.

The three or four days Mother's Day trip turned out to be a time of bonding for my mother and me

We rented a car and drove to San Francisco and other major site seeing spots. Jeff introduced us to several of his friends'.

The last day of our trip, Jeff's personality changed; he became very agitated. As usual, I became the target of his attack. From experience, I knew that something had happened. His behavior signal that he had done something wrong. His defense included shifting the blame to someone else. I could not identify the problem, but I just knew that our last day in California would end on a sour note!

The plan for getting us to the airport included one of Jeff's friends driving us there. After the three of us piled into the rental car, we drove to the friend's house. Jeff was driving, and when he pulled up to his friend's apartment, he got out and went to the door. A young man came out, and he and Jeff exchanged a few words. Upon getting in the car, Jeff informed us that his friend would not be able to take us to the airport. I began to ask some questions. Jeff's reaction to my questions surprised my mother and me. He became loud and almost out of control.

He jumped out of the car and walked away. Lucky for me, we were in the area of the hotel where we stayed. I drove back to the hotel and called the rental car company to come and pick up the car. My mother and I made reservations to catch the next shuttle bus from the hotel to the airport.

As I prepared to pay for our trip to the airport, I realized that I was short on cash. However, I was okay because I kept a hundred dollar bill tucked away in my wallet. The hundred-dollar bill was gone! It all became clear. At some point, Jeff had gotten into my purse the night before, on Mother's Day.

I vowed that I would ultimately walk away from Jeff. When we arrived at the airport, I called his barrack, and a young man answered the phone. After telling him who I was, he said,

"Oh, hi, Ms. Dove, this is Troy, Jeff's friend. We met the other day."

"Is Jeff there?"

"Yes, ma'am, I will get him."

"Hello?" I jumped right on Jeff. *How could you take money from my wallet, yak, yak, yak?* He did not say a word, but I could hear him breathing on the phone. Throughout our trials, he had never, to my knowledge, taken money from me. After returning home, I was determined to cut him off. We had no contact with each other for months.

On one occasion, while praying, I began to pray that God would start to teach me how to balance my relationship with my son. I did not want to cut him off completely, but yet, I knew that for my psychological well being, I needed to learn how to set boundaries with our relationship.

While praying, I was directed by the Holy Spirit to Matthew, the seventh chapter. After turning to the scripture reading, I was shocked at the opening verse: "Do not judge, or you too will be judged." At that moment, I had a flashback to a conversation that Jeff and I had on one occasion during a heated discussion. I said to him, "It's almost as if you do not have a conscience. Do you not care how your behavior affects others?" Looking at me with tears in his eyes, he said, "How do you know how I feel? How do you know I don't care?" After that conversation, I began to realize that people who have addictive behaviors, do care; it's the addiction that doesn't feel or care.

That day, I read the entire seventh chapter of Matthew, but I began to focus and meditate on verses 1-5:

> "Do not judge, or you too will be judged. For in the same way you judge others, you will be judged, and with the measure you use, it will be measured to you.
>
> Why do you look at the speck of sawdust in your brother's eye and pay no attention to

the plank in your own eye? How can you say to your brother, 'Let me take the speck out of your eye,' when all the time there is a plank in your eye? You hypocrite, first take the plank out of your eye, and then you will see clearly to remove the speck from your brother's eye."

NIV – Matthew 7:1-5

I began to ask some serious questions about my behavior. *Lord, how had I been judging Jeff's behavior? Did I see it as something that he could change? Had my focus been on Jeff rather than the addiction and what it does to people? What was my motive for wanting him to make a 180 degree turn around? Could it be that I was more interested in "saving face" for my good?* Most assuredly, I did not want my extended family, friends, and colleagues to know my real suffering, but more importantly, my son's pain. What would they think of me as a mother? Did I find it easier to magnify Jeff's faults while excusing my own? As a parent, did I have a responsibility to educate myself on the many "social ills" of our society that my children would face, especially during those formative years of adolescence? Did I take pride that I had worked myself and children up to middle class status, thereby feeling secure that we had overcome drugs and other destructive things in our society?

After the encounter of judging others, I ran across a reading that changed me forever. The title of the passage is: <u>Let Go!</u> (Author Unknown).

Let go!

to "let go" does not mean to stop caring, it means
I can't do it for someone else.
to "let go" is not to cut myself off, it's the realization
I can't control another.
to "let go" is not to enable, but to allow learning
from natural consequences.
to "let go" is to admit powerlessness, which means
the outcome is not in my hands.
to "let go" is not to try to change or blame another,
it's to make the most of myself.
to "let go" is not to care for, but to care about.
to "let go" is not to fix, but to be supportive.
to "let go" is not to judge, but to allow another to
be a human being.
to "let go" is not to be in the middle arranging all the
outcomes but to allow others to affect their destinies.
to "let go" is not to be protective, it's to permit
another to face reality.
to "let go" is not to nag, scold or argue, but instead to
search out my own shortcomings and correct them.
to "let go" is not to adjust everything to my desires
but to take each day as it comes, and cherish myself
in it.
to "let go" is not to criticize and regulate anybody
but to try to become what I dream I can be.
to "let go" is not to regret the past, but to grow and
live for the future.
to "let go" is to fear less and love more.

CHAPTER FOURTEEN

"Grace"

During seminary, I began to seek and search out "religious truth" for myself. As I started this journey, my perception of God's relationship with humankind rested on God's "Grace,"; a grace that is extended to all. After discovering the concept of grace, I began to accept Jeff, and even myself, in a new light, for grace came to mean to me "the free unconditional love and favor of God toward all humankind." I believe that God's grace is found throughout nature. Therefore this Christian doctrine upholds a belief that God's grace is all around us and in us. Now I know that God does love all people, no matter what, even those who deny God exist.

God's grace does not depend on our good works, merits, or righteousness. I now understand that grace is free, and when we respond to God's grace with a deep sense of humility, we begin to humble ourselves before God.

Even before we come to understand and submit to God's grace, God protects us through prevenient grace, which is divine love that surrounds all humanity and precedes all of our conscious impulses. God sits back and waits for us to accept His unconditional love.

With this new awareness, I began to question my unconditional love for my son. I knew that I loved him, but was it, unconditional love? No! My love was conditional, based on control. I thought that if he would only do as I said, his life would be so much better. I loved Jeff, but I was more concerned with my hurts, and my wants. I soon began to understand that I needed to step back and let God's prevenient grace continue to prevail, up to the point where he would cry out for help that would go beyond anything that I could do for him.

One day, as I prayed, I cried out, "God, please protect Jeff from bodily harm or death. Let him come to accept your grace."The spirit within responded with, "I will spare him."

Society dictates, if parents work hard, teach their children basic rules of life, and provide the necessities for their children, they will grow up and go to college and become productive citizens. According to society's law, these same children will one day obey the rules and regulations, stay out of trouble, and make their parents very proud.

To detour from the path would undoubtedly mean that the parent did not do an outstanding job! When parents feel that they have not done a "good job" in raising a child, they may also think that the rules were broken, and consequently, the parent failed the test.

As a parent, for so long, I felt as if I had failed. I was not a good mother, and if I was not a good mother. The laws of society were violated. Therefore, grace could not be found within me to love unconditionally, not even myself. The rules of society became more important than God's Grace. As I continued to study and reflect on the concept of grace, I soon understood that the same grace that had been given to me by God was the same grace that I should extend to Jeff. As an individual, he had a right to discover and form his identity. I began to step back and let go slowly.

Without realizing it, I eventually comprehended that throughout the years, God had been amazingly timely in responding to me as I prayed for Jeff. I began to understand that maybe God had something more in mind for Jeff other than my desires for him. Rather than changing the circumstances, God began to change my heart.

CHAPTER FIFTEEN

A Song of Praise

After getting out of the military, Jeff came back to Georgia to live; he moved in with Lee and me.

After the first week, I realized that the white elephant was making its way back into my house, and I was not going to allow that to happen. Lee and I discussed creating a timeframe on how long he could live with us. We agreed on a month. But after about ten days, I realized that I had to "let go" because things were not working out. I called a family meeting for the three of us and informed Jeff that he needed to be out by the end of the week. Again, I got that look. Teary eyes that said, I let her down again.

He moved into an apartment for about three months. One day, he came by the house with a carload of clothes. He informed me that he was evicted from his apartment and was on his way to Florida to stay with his grandmother.

I called my mother to give her an advanced warning, and like always, she took the news very calmly. Shortly after moving to Florida, Jeff contacted a junior college basketball coach at Abraham Baldwin College in Tifton, Georgia. The coach had visited Jeff when he was playing basketball in high school. At that time, he invited us down to visit the school. We never made the trip.

To my surprise, Jeff got himself admitted to the college and began playing college basketball. At twenty-one, he was viewed as the older man on the team. Once, when the team played in Atlanta, I went to the game. His high school coach in Jacksonville was correct; Jeff had the potential to be a great player.

Tifton was only about 160 miles from where my mother lived in Lake City, Florida. On some weekends, Jeff would go and stay with her. Unfortunately, after the first year, he did not return to college. He moved back in with his grandmother.

For years, I protected my mother from the harsh realities of Jeff's addictive behavior. The mood swings that went along with the addictions could strain the most stable relationships.

As the addictive behavior began to rear its ugly head, my mother became aware of the problems that go along with addictions, even though his actions were not directed toward her, she soon became aware of the ugly byproducts of the disease.

Through it all, my mother continued to offer support. I called it "grandmother's grace." She never condemned or judged him. She always provided support by way of kind words or deeds. Even though at times he would get an apartment, he would end up back at his grandmother's house. I would try to encourage her not to let him return, but she always provided a place for him to stay.

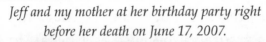

Jeff and my mother at her birthday party right before her death on June 17, 2007.

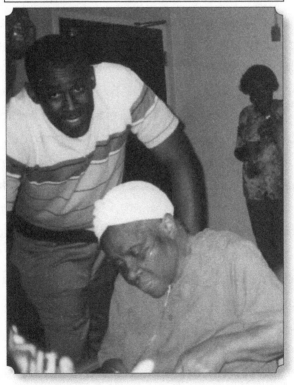

As time passes, I began to see a slight change in Jeff's behavior, but there continued to be internal warfare. He would make two steps forward and four backward. Throughout these difficult times, there were no close encounters with the law. I have always been grateful that he did not violate the rules of society to the point of having a severe criminal record because I knew that if he did, he would have an even deeper hole to climb up.

During this time, I became more convinced that Jeff would turn his life around. I was sure that he would become a preacher, but I believe that only God and I had this assurance because as I began to tell other family members about my revelation, they would look at me as if to say, "Yeah, right, and I'm going to fly to the moon."

Even though our relationship was strained, there would be times when we would talk to each other from the heart. During these times, he would be very open and candid with me about his drug use and other activities. On one occasion, as we talked, I asked him what types of drugs he used. He said, "You name it, and I've tried it." Also, he added that by all accounts, he should have been dead many years ago. My heart wept for my son, a young man in his early twenties confessing that he had lived a life that by all accounts should have caused him a premature death. "Thank you, God, for divine grace!"

There was a young preacher who moved to Lake City, where Jeff was living with my mother. This young preacher's focus was working with the youth and young adults in the community. One day, out of the blue, I called him and told him that I had a son living there, and I would be grateful if he would stop by my mother's house and talk with him. As it turned out, my telephone call paid off. Shortly after that, he introduced himself to Jeff and invited him to church. At some point, Jeff took him up on the invitation and started attending the church, and later became a member. Gradually he began to work with the young people in the church. He became an instant success. They loved him! He could identify with their struggles, and his heart was sincere.

As he began to work in the church, his innate leadership abilities began to surface. He organized a citywide back to school party for children in the community who needed school supplies. At the first gathering, he invited me to come and speak to the group. As I looked out at the young faces staring back at me, I was moved. I prayed for divine protection for all of them, especially from the evils of drugs that were beginning to destroy generations of our youth.

Just as things began to level off for Jeff, the pastor was reassigned to another church. I was hoping that Jeff would continue to work in the church. Later, a replacement pastor was appointed. Who, in my opinion, was above reproach, a man after God's heart. He was a man full of grace and integrity. In addition to being an outstanding preacher and pastor, he was an exceptional educator in the community, and he was appointed to be a principal of one of the elementary schools. He restored and achieved healing to the church, and church membership grew. The community fell in love with him.

Also, His wife was an ordained minister who worked alongside him.

He and Jeff became instant friends, and he became Jeff's role model. He took Jeff under his wings. I began to see not only a change in Jeff's relationship with God but with other people. Even the way he dressed changed. He became a carbon copy of his mentor, suits, starched shirts, and shined shoes. I know that the pastor received a platoon of negative feedback about Jeff in the church because of small-town gossip; however, he never wavered in his support of Jeff. He continued to groom him and shepherd him into the house of God.

Later, Jeff enrolled in the community college and began to be more involved in the community and church. In addition to being a free spirit, he also has a heart for social justice issues. He became involved with the student organization at the college.

The pastor began to give him more responsibility in the church, and Jeff's confidence began to soar. On one occasion, I asked him if he felt called to preach. After pondering the question for a few seconds, he shook his head using the universal no, non-verbal cue.

Fighting drugs

ABAC BASKETBALL player Jeffrey Dove, from Florida, writes an anti-alcohol message Monday on a temporary brick wall erected at the college. Messages written on the wall helped kick off Drug Awareness Week at the local college. (Gazette Photo by E.L. Hubbard)

CHAPTER SIXTEEN

A Double Blessing, A Time to Cross Over

A s I neared the finish line at Candler School of Theology to receive my Master's of Divinity Degree, I became excited about the possibilities of preaching and working in the church.

While in seminary, I served as a student pastor at my home church in Atlanta, Cascade United Methodist Church. In this position, I was responsible for the singles ministry, teaching Sunday school, coordinating clergy retreats, and serving as block community clergy where I was in charge of the spiritual needs of the group. I was acquiring much experience.

After my initial discussion with Lee about my desire to pursue ordination, I made a vow that I would not bring it up again. I decided to win him over by example. I kept a low profile and continued to honor him. Soon, we both began to grow spiritually. I was eager to share with Lee all that I was learning in seminary.

Lee became my biggest supporter. He started attending church with me regularly, and we began to have home Bible study together. Whenever asked to speak or preach, he would be there sitting on the front seat. As I continued working on my seminary degree, I served several other small churches as a local senior pastor. Lee was right there, becoming very active in each church. Congregation members loved him. Although he was a man of few words, his very inviting personality would win anyone over.

Graduation day finally arrived. I was excited, Lee was thrilled, and my mother was delighted. She came up from Florida to attend graduation. As I sat through the ceremony, I remember my promise to God. "If you want me to preach, you will need to open doors." I've learned not to challenge God unless you are willing to follow through with God's plan. Doors may open; however, we must do the labor to complete the job. The journey of becoming a female pastor was not easy, but God opened doors that I felt had been locked with a deadbolt.

During my seminary years, I came to realize that Jesus was the best advocate for women because he went against the traditions of society and culture by recognizing, embracing women, and encouraging women. Jesus had a genuine concern for women during a period in history when women had very little input. Frequently, his twelve apostles rebuked him for his kindness and unconditional love for women.

For example, I was and continue to be moved by the kindness shown by Jesus to the woman mentioned in the Bible (Mark 5:26). This woman had been rejected by society because of an illness that she suffered. She had gone to many doctors, spending all of her money to find a cure. The disease, an issue of blood, had invaded her body for twelve years. Because of this, she was seen as unclean by society's law. Therefore she was restricted from having contact with others. For whatever reason, she decided to go against the rules of society. On hearing that Jesus would be in the area, she made plans to go to the gathering. She believed that if she could touch his garment, she would be made whole again. She pushed her way through the crowd, and after touching Jesus, she immediately felt the healing power of Jesus flowing through her body. Jesus knew that someone had reached out for help. "Who touched me?" said Jesus (Mark 5:31). The woman came forward and told Jesus all about her long-suffering. Jesus healed her.

I needed to touch the hem of Jesus' garment for the sake of my son. Jeff had suffered for many years, with the disease of drug addiction. As I continued to pray, I became stronger. I was able to stand firm.

After being mentored by Rev. Kracher in the church for almost two years, Jeff began to be more serious about his work in the church. One Saturday afternoon, the phone rang. "Hello mama, this is Jeff." "Rev. Kracher and I talked about me becoming a preacher. I believe you are correct. God is calling me to preach!" I almost dropped the phone. He ended the conversation by saying, "I will preach in April." "Jeff, that's only four weeks away."

When Lee arrived home, I met him at the door, grinning from ear to ear. "I come bearing good news. We will have two ministries in the family, mother, and son!"

I called my mother and we began to plan a grand celebration. We invited friends and family from far and near to the ceremony, Jeff's initial sermon. Anthony hesitated to commit to coming from Maryland to Florida for the event. Once again, Lee stepped in, without telling me, and called Anthony and had a man-to-man informing him that he could not miss this event. I later learned that Anthony committed without further delay. Lee and I arrived at my mother's house two days early on that Friday before the big day. Anthony came, and we had a wonderful family reunion.

That Sunday morning was brisk and bright, not a cloud in the sky. The family began to arrive; family stories were shared, especially those relating to Jeff. "Man, I can't believe that you are going to be a preacher." "Boy, your mama kept the faith." Somebody said, "hey, Rev." and laughter filled the house.

Through the laughter and play, I slipped off into the backyard and stood under the huge oak tree. Looking up toward the clear blue sky, I said, "thank you, God."

I knew that this was only the beginning of Jeff's journey to becoming an ordained AME pastor. First, he had to get his four-year degree, and then seminary. The door opened, now the work would begin.

Rev. Kracher stood up to introduce Jeff, "I present to you a man called by God." As the 6'5" figure stood up tall, shoulders straight, my heart leaped for joy. My heart said- a double blessing. "Good evening family and friends, thanks for coming today. My sermon's title is 'It's Time to Cross Over.'"

CPSIA information can be obtained
at www.ICGtesting.com
Printed in the USA
BVHW031653210520
580105BV00002B/2/J